HE'S *My* FATHER

ELDER TONY McDOWELL

ISBN 979-8-89345-219-8 (paperback)
ISBN 979-8-89345-220-4 (digital)

Christian Faith Publishing
832 Park Avenue
Meadville, PA 16335
www.christianfaithpublishing.com

Change Me

Change me from the inside out
Change me
Let there be no doubt
That I'm a new man
From head to toe
My direction has changed
I now know where to go
I've set my affections on things up above
Where Christ sitteth
And I know I'm loved
He loves me and I'll never be the same
Now that the Son has written
My name

Trying to Make It In

Sometimes I wonder if I'll make it in
Living in a world laden with sin
Living among sinners is hard for a saint
With all the dos and don'ts, and the things you can't
Temptations, trials on every hand, it's difficult for the moral
and righteous to stand
Can't lust, can't lie, can't even steal
Because all those things are against God's will
Crime and chaos seem to be the norm
Hurricanes, tornadoes, so much destruction from the storms
It's a beautiful world that God made,
But if Satan wasn't in it, we'd have better days
But God has prepared a better place than this
If we remain faithful, we won't miss
Streets of gold, gates of pearl, there's so
much more in this new world
No more sorrow, no more pain, we will live
there forever and He will reign

A Father Tears

A father's tears are warm yet cold
A father's tears that touch the soul
When a son dies who's not yet old
When a friend cries it doesn't console
There are tears of joy and tears of pain
But when a son dies there are tears you can't sustain
A father's tears can be wiped away
But the scars are there day after day
Oh, what pain you feel, when a loved one is gone
But God will give you strength and courage to carry on

Jesus
My Superhero

My superhero, John saw him from afar
His arrival was announced by a shining star
Three came to Bethlehem where the Baby lay
Laying in a manger peaceful and dry
My superhero grew up to be a Man
Holding the sins of the world in his hand
On the cross he would die,
Only to rise again to ascend on high
Death, hell, and the grave couldn't hold him down
The Pharisees and Pilate were all astound
When they rolled back the stone and nothing was found
The angel cried "He's not here, he's
ascended far into the atmosphere"
My superhero will return again to gather all the saints
And make one final stand, a stand against the devil
For all the world to see, my superhero rescued me

We Win

Lord, I'm weary
My soul is in despair
Tossed, battered, and bruised
It seems no one cares
No strength, no might
But I can't give up the fight
Here, is where I dig in
I must get some resolve
My strength is in you
It comes from above
My joy, my peace
I must contend for the faith
It's an all-out war
I can't make any mistakes
The devil is trying to kill me
But the Holy Spirit is on my side
Goodness and mercy are there as my guide
I hear the Lord saying, my son be strong
And all the saints in heaven
Cheering me to still fight on
I'm feeling stronger now, my joy just kicked in
Blessed assurance, I know, I know, I can win

Giving You Back Control

As I search my heart and mind
Not liking what I see
As I look in the rearview mirror
All I see is me
Like a car coming out of control
Running in and out lanes
No regard for anyone else's safety
Driving like a person insane
As he passed by, I got a glance
Seeing a reflection of myself
I didn't have a chance
My life had gone before me
Leaving me behind
In its path wreckage and ruins
All I could find
A life out of control
Because God's not in the plan
That's the end results, when things are left in man's hand
So I'm giving you back control, saying "Yes, I surrender"
I'm no match for your sovereignty, I'm no contender
Because you know what's best for me, my life is in your hand
The Bible is our roadmap, it's your master plan

God's Creation

Such beauty, such grace, such poetry in motion
These are the wonders of the seas and the oceans
So He made man, in His image he stood
God said to Jesus, "I wish he'd move, I wish he could"
So He breathed into his nostrils
He became a living soul, gave him authority
and power and made him whole
He also made woman, took a rib from Adam's side
Made him a helpmate, in her he could confide
Animals, birds and bees, the flowers and the trees
It's God's creation, whether big or small
The greatest thing about it is that He loves them all

I Saw the Light

It happened a long, long time ago
I was traveling down this long, winding, dusty road
When suddenly a light shined from heaven down
It encompassed me all around
Then suddenly a voice I heard
As he so softly said
"Son of man, do my will"
And I said "Yes, Lord," as I trembled still
"But, Lord, what shall I do?"
"Go tell the world my love is true
Tell them I'm coming soon
It may be morning, night or noon
I sent my Son to die on the cross
I sent my Son to save that which was lost"

Speak Softly

Speak softly words of encouragement
Speak softly words of strength
Speak softly to turn anger away
Speak softly so you can come together
Before the end of the day
Speak it with compassion
Speak it with love
Because wisdom comes from up above
S p e a k, s o f t l y
Can't you sense the hush?
Speak softly
Don't be in a rush
Because words are alive and they do hurt
Be quick to say I'm sorry before it's too late
S p e a k, s o f t l y
Turn wrath away
Speak softly live to love another day

The Moon and the Sea

The moon and the sea
Here's you and here's me
On a romantic and starry night
Our love shines bright
As we walk hand in hand
Leaving our footprints in the sand
It's incredible to see
The moon and the sea

While I'm on My Journey Home

There is a place I'm destined to be
There is a place prepared just for me
While I'm on my journey, my journey home
There are things I must do, things I can't prolong
We must preach the gospel each and every day
We must reach the lost and show them the way
I must visit the sick while I have time
There is no time to rest, there is no time to whine
Visit those in prison too, there is so much
And so little time to do
Heal the sick, raise the dead
Do all the things that Jesus said
While I'm on my journey home
There is no time to wander, no time to roam

From Poverty to the Penthouse
Rise, Penny, Rise

Rise, Penny, rise from the bottom to the top
From the playgrounds of Memphis
That little round ball you rocked
Day after day until the day was done
You mastered it, you crafted it until one day you won
Sunup to sundown until the early morning rise
It became your closest companion as it lay by your side
You knew one day in the back of your mind
That you would leave all this madness behind
From grade school to college, you had a plan
To play in the NBA and be the number one man
From poverty to the penthouse to fortune and fame
Rise, Penny, rise until we meet again

"One Moment Away from Eternity"

It's sad to say some won't make it in
Too proud, won't repent
They'd rather live in sin
They had a choice the straight and narrow way
They choose the other called the broad way
If you're reading this, you still have time
To have a change of heart and a change of mind
Our lives are described as a bubble on the water
Here today and gone tomorrow
Good days, bad days, never the same
Always mixed with sunshine and rain
The Bible says hell is hot
The rich man agreed
"Don't come down here, don't follow me"
Lazarus, he's got it made
He's with Abraham, cooling in the shade
One drop of water, is all I need
To quench my thirst, to let off some steam
One moment from eternity
We only have one chance
Life passes before us, just like a glance
Stop, repent before it's too late
Give Jesus your heart, please don't wait

Just Telling the Truth

It's Monday morning, it's time to go to work
With retirement around the corner
I don't want to be late
Thirty years—it's been a long time
Providing for a wife, home and children
Trying to maintain a peace of mind
Watching the children grow up and go away
Watching the hair on my head turn gray
My steps are slower now than ever before
But my mind is sharper, stronger, now I understand more
Life has taken a toll on this body of mine
No time to pout, no time to whine
There's still work to do and so little time
Week after week, it's all a rewind
Soon it will be over, my day will be done
Relaxing on a cruise ship, bathing in the sun

God's Hand

Since the beginning, when time didn't exist
You stretched forth your hand
Created something out of the mist
Sun and moon, you hung in the sky
Dividing light from darkness from on high
Darkness was pushed out of the way
To bring sunlight and the dawning of a brand-new day
Oceans were formed, rivers were made
Mountains, valleys, and waterfalls cascade
Fruits were budding from the trees
Ready to reproduce itself from its own seeds
But you didn't leave out man, you scooped him from the ground
With the palm of your hand
All the animals in the land, they also were a part of your master plan
God's hand created it all
Winter, spring, summer, and fall

Breathe in Me

Breathe in me, revive me again
My soul faints from the weight of sin
Call forth the winds from the north, south, east, and west
Cause these bones to live
My soul needs rest
Tired of the struggle, don't want to give in
Send forth your Spirit so I can win
I'm tired and weary, awaiting his return
I'm patiently waiting, my soul does yearn
Breathe in me I feel a refreshing
Holy Spirit, come
I'm in need of a blessing

Imagine

Imagine a city far, far away
Imagine joy and laughter, where children play
Imagine no more heartache and pain
No more selfish men out for selfish gain
Imagine a city of pure gold, crystal clear waters
Where men never grow old
Trees for the healing of the nations
Imagine no more nuclear bombs and nuclear waste stations
Imagine a city for you and for me
Imagine a city where all God's children will be free
Just imagine

I Was the One
(Whom No One Ever Knew)

I was the one whose clothes were tattered and torn
I was the one who was so ashamed, and wished I was never born
I was the one who sat in the back of the
class whom no one ever knew
I was the one who was disinterested and didn't have a clue
No one took interest, no one considered that I wanted to learn too
I was in the back of the class, no one ever knew
"Hey, you, what's your name?" Too quiet and shy to say
It's been over forty years, and still it haunts me today
In my family, a child was seen and not heard
In my home, that was the last word
From grade school until high school, it remained the same
I was in the room, but no one knew my name
But that'll be okay, God gave me a choice, to
remain silent or choose to have a voice
So I write poetry, I have a lot to say
I can express myself, in my own way
For you out there who may have felt the same
Just pick up a pen, just start by writing your name

My Best Days Are Ahead

Sitting quietly in this room
Awaiting the angel who's coming soon
I've been preparing for this all my life
I'm not afraid—afraid to die
God promised me
Streets of gold, gates of pearls
There's nothing like it in this old world
Walls of jasper, sapphire, and beryl
All precious stones, there's so many layers
No more sickness, no more disease
Not even a cough, not even a sneeze
No more pain nor sorrow
There will be a better tomorrow
A robe, a ring, a crown on my head
My best days are just up ahead

Just Having Fun

On the playgrounds
Children on the swings
Climbing the monkey bars
How long has it been?
Reflecting back, on days gone by
So long ago, oh how time flies
Remembering when I played in the sand
Making mud pies with my friends
Just children having fun
Enjoying a carefree life in the sun
Rainy days, the fun didn't end
Floating popsicle sticks
Along the curb's bend
Bike rides, swimming pools all summer long
Not wanting it to end, not wanting to go home
But tomorrow would come, as today would end
Just having fun, me and my friends

She's a Very Special Lady

She's a very special lady, so genuine and so true
She has a heart of gold, how precious are you
More precious than silver, rubies, diamonds, and pearls
With a smile so infectious it brightens the world
Warm soft lips, black coarse hair, she's a radiant beauty
That doesn't compare
Her arms reach out to hold you with a warm embrace
Holding you so tightly, there's no other place
Eyes of compassion, loving and true
She's a very special lady
Oh how I love you.
To my loving wife
Norma

Redeeming Love

Once upon a time, man was lost
Shackled by sin
To be redeemed at a great cost
Held captive by the wicked one
Angry and rebellious, he was once a son
Now the story begins in the garden one day
Man and woman were going about their merry way
Suddenly, the serpent appeared
Saying "Take, eat, you won't surely die
Everything God told you was a lie"
She ate, he ate, their eyes came open wide
"We're naked," they both replied
Hiding themselves, one from the other
Now the union is broken
Can't commune with each other
God walks through the garden, it's quiet and still
"Adam, where are you?" "I'm naked!" he shrilled

Now God's plan goes into effect
The serpent is cursed, man is shipwrecked
Toiling day after day in the hot sun
Trying to master the soil, it always won
Women bearing children always near death's door
Pain and suffering
It would be that way forever more
But that's not how the story ends
Feast, burnt offering
Could not atone for sin
Generation after generation, sin would prevail
It looked like man was destined for hell
Jesus said, "Prepare me a body, starting today
I'll remove the curse and open up a better way"
Jesus was born, God's only Son defeated the enemy
Now victory is won

Right Now, I'm Free

Right now, I'm free
Ain't no pressure on me
On a mountain high above
Surrounded by God's precious love
Great Smoky Mountains, Gatlinburg, Tennessee
What a wonder for your eyes to see
Great people in the midst
Life couldn't get no better than this
My mind is clear
No stress on me
I thank God right now, I'm free

He's My Father

A man big and strong, who's gone through life broken and torn.
He's been my provider all life long.
What will I do without him now that he's gone?
There's so much pain I feel in my heart
I know Mother is lonely now that you're apart
He's my father, full of love and cheer.
He had a wonderful smile you could see from ear to ear.
Through joy, laughter, and pain, his sense
of humor, he always maintained.
Though life seemed to always give him a hard time,
someway, somehow, he had peace of mind.
He's my father, there's none like him in all the world
He was one of earth's secrets and now one of heaven's pearls.
I miss you

In memory of
Willie Davis McDowell Sr. August 23, 1932–February 23, 1982

It's Raining Today

It's raining today
It's dark, cloudy, and gray
The streets are wet and it's cold
But don't lose heart
God's still in control
Some days are filled with sunshine and rain
But don't despair
God knows your pain
He always knows
Just what to do
He sends a word of comfort to bring us through
It's raining, but the sun will shine
Don't worry, you will be fine
He sends comfort through a word or a song
Before you know it, you will be humming along
A song like
"Amazing grace, how sweet the sound that saved
A wretch like me
I once was lost, but now I'm found
Blind but now I see"
It's raining today, but the Son is on the throne
He's smiling, and saying, "My child
It won't be long"

Don't Let This World Get You Down

When the pressures of life get you down
Don't greet the world with a frown
Turn it upside down
Because in the end
We're gonna win
Don't let this world get you down
Maybe you're feeling a little downhearted and blue
And you don't know just what to do
I have a Friend who loves one and all
He'll be there when you call
Never too busy and never late
His name is Jesus, he's a very good mate
So when times get hard
He's always around
So don't let this world get you down

A Tennessee Morning

A gentle summer breeze blows across the land
The warmth of the sun on the back of your hand
Dewdrops glistened on the grass below
Flowers blossom, you can almost hear them grow
The leaves on the trees are brightly green
Birds chirping, how loudly they sing
Bees, hummingbirds sing their song
There's harmony in the air all day long
Squirrels leaping from tree to tree
Some even flying, they seem so free
The dawning of a new day, and I'm feeling fine
I look toward the heavens, and I have a volunteer state of mind
It's a Tennessee morning, I'm sipping cold iced tea
Sitting on the back porch, my baby and me

God Help Me Find My Way

Stumbling in the dark
Can't find my way home
Wondering in the earth
I feel so alone
I'm that child again
Lost and afraid
Riding my bike
With no one to aid
It's getting late
And the tears are beginning to fall
I'm riding and riding
And mother can't hear my call
I'm just around the corner
A few blocks from home
It seems like an eternity
That I've been gone
Nothings familiar
So I begin to pray
God help me, find my way
Childlike faith
Will bring you thru
Theirs home in the distance
An I knew
My prayer had been answered
I'm glad to say
Home sweet home
Never again will i stray

So if ever again
I'm lost and afraid
I'll simply pray
God help me, find my way

About the Author

I am married to an amazing beautiful woman named Norma Jean. The Lord has blessed us to be married forty-four years. We have three lovely daughters, Kimvenley, Kamisha, and Toni; and we also have a host of grandchildren and great-grandchildren. I'm a graduate of Booker T. Washington High School. I've worked for the US postal service for thirty years. I'm an ordained elder, poet, singer, songwriter, and author. I pray that my poems be an inspiration and blessing to all those who read them. Thank you and God's blessing be upon you.